Smart Life University:

Your Master Key to Success

Haywood Barber

PUBLISHED BY BLUE ARTISTS, LLC

This publication is designed to provide accurate and authoritative information in regard to the subject matter covered. It is sold with the understanding that the publisher is not engaged in rendering legal, accounting, or other professional service. If legal advice or other expert assistance is required, the services of a competent professional person should be sought.

CONTENTS

PREFACE

In this book, Haywood Barber answers an age old question that many of us have been searching for. It's something that has us up late and rising early to try to finally realize. We all want it. Dream, study, wish, want, wait, and if we are lucky ultimately … we find and keep it!

What's that? It's Success! The kind of success that isn't fleeting but lasting and that you can build on. Well, "Smart Life University: Your Master Key to Success", is your access to that level of pure, repetitive, unlimited success.

In this powerful book, Haywood Barber, Master Trainer, Real Estate Powerhouse, and Champion for people lays out a path and formula to have success in any industry, with any demographic, or geographical location. His track record for being a king-maker and giving instruction to thousands

while on their path to greatness speaks for itself. What's even more impressive is that now he has chosen to share those secrets and insights with you in order to help elevate his dedication to paying it forward at an even greater degree.

As you read through pages of "Smart Life University: Your Master Key to Success", you will find that word by word, step by step, and principle by principle, Haywood is giving you the blueprint to finally live your dreams. Whether your passion is real estate investing, making Raggedy Anne dolls, or building a rocket ship, these lessons are tried and true stepping stones to building a solid foundation for success delivered in a simple and digestible fashion.

The notes and easily applicable knowledge you acquire from "Smart Life University: Your Master Key to Success" should often be revisited, applied, and revisited again. Its timeless information will serve as a go-to for you in your business and personal life for many years to come.

One of the primary things that Mr. Barber focuses on is the power that you possess to determine your own outcomes. Through his stories, examples, and teachings, you will be able to see yourself and redirect your thought, behavior, and purposeful actions to overcome the toughest of odds. Having come from humble beginnings and recreating himself and his path, Mr. Barber is well aware of

what it's like to live on both sides of the fence. It is that knowledge which gives him the ability to relate to you, the reader, no matter what your starting point or when in your life you pick up this treasure.

The people that read books like "Smart Life University: Your Master Key to Success" are seeking the ways to win in life. In this book, you will receive the "Master Key" to unlock new experiences, ideas, perspectives, and possibilities that are needed to make the adjustments necessary to go to the next level. Mr. Barber's mentoring will give you the tools to reach your biggest and most desired goals.

You picked up this book because you are already on a journey and you have a hunger to push the envelope and become the best you possible. You are brave and willing to do whatever it takes to master your live. This will help you. This is what you have been looking for. He wrote this book just for you. You are on your way!

Read it, embrace it, apply it, live it... and get ready to live a life you never even knew was possible.

Dr. Lola Thompson

Author, Entrepreneurial Mentor, and Coach

Boundless Education

MINDSET

My name is Haywood Barber and I am the founder of Smart Life University. My biggest passion in life is to coach, teach, and train people on how to have a better life. My sole purpose is to help people. I love people just as much as I love myself. I think that is a key point that when we love ourselves deeply it's very simple and very easy to love others. I do. I have a strong passion for people and seeing people grow. What I know about people is that there's more inside them than they're full aware of, as I've learned about myself.

Smart Life University is simply what the name

implies. It is actually a smart way of conveying truly good information about how to have a good life, to have a better life, to make things simpler in your life, and to be smart about life. It was a strong passion for me even before the name came around. The name just seemed to fall in my lap.

The most important reason why I was compelled to create Smart Life was to help so many people. The Haywood Barber writing this book is from the projects of New York City. My personal development was the result of a team of people that worked independent from each other. There were just so many people instrumental in my life. I can tell you from my early youth the people that were instrumental in my life, that made me a better person, that made me good enough an expert at being who I am and honing in on my craft. This team of people came so early into my life that I didn't really understand it. It wasn't until 15 years ago that I realized that's what made me, me.

Mindset is a philosophy of thought patterns that help us get from A to B. Where we are right now is the result of a mindset. A better mindset is developed through a process of simple small changes.

One thing I've learned while teaching and training over the last 25 years is I don't want people to take big leaps in trying to change their lives because the likelihood of success is small. I know most people are already aware of this. Even when you start an exercise regimen you have a tendency to go out there overdo it then the next day you're hurting. You need Tylenol and you quit or you get outside your plan.

What we have found at Smart Life is that we want to just show you how to develop patterns of mindset in small increments so that they become habits. When they become habits, they become a regimen. When that regimen is engrained in you, the groove is in your brain; it becomes a part of your Smart Life.

A better mindset helps you to see more, to be more focused and then be able to be more receptive to the ideas and how to use them. A lot of times people say "I had that idea years ago". Of course you did but because of your current mindset at the time it was just a fleeting thought. If I can get your mindset to be receptive, that idea might be your Bill Gates inspiration moment.

As you get to know me through Smart Life University, you'll get to know a big part of my history. I've been teaching and training all of my life. Even when I was a car salesman, I was teaching and training on the sales floor. They told me I was a natural because I was a natural leader. I always wanted to give of myself that's who I am.

That's what Smart Life University is. It's a platform

of giving. I can speak to audiences for hours. I've never spoke in front of 1,000 people though. It's a goal of mine. I always could talk in front of audiences.

I wanted to put together a nice series in my early days of teaching and training in personal

development and real estate investing so I got a studio. I had someone that was going to direct me, with producers and everything. I have to tell you I failed. I could not produce and perform in front of cameras, and lights. I was a disaster. When I say a disaster, I couldn't do it. You know, you would think that a guy that could public speak, teach and train hundreds of people could do this. I did a horrible job. I just couldn't do it. I had stage fright from the lights and the cameras.

And guess what? I had to analyze myself and realize what I still had to overcome. I had to use my mindset to say that that disaster, that setback is only a setup for a comeback. Now I can talk in front of cameras, lights, the guys doing the action, with the powder in my face, and everybody telling me to fix my tie. It's a great thing.

I overcame my mindset but I didn't take big chunks. The tendency always is I want to change everything right away. Even that story I just told you, I was devastated. I was beating up on myself most of that day for not being able to overcome the poor job I was doing. I wanted to fix it right then on the spot because that's who I am. I want to fix things now.

I have learned over the years you can't eat an elephant one large bite at a time. You also can't eat an elephant with just a few bites. You've got to take many smaller bites. That's the best way to do it, take your time, but stay on task.

So small incremental changes helped me change my

mindset. That's what I suggest that everyone tries. You try small goals at first and then you will achieve your goals. Make small changes as you go along. Don't try to fix it all immediately, fix it bit-by-bit one day at a time. Meaningful goals take time.

Mindset is a thought process. It's a pattern of thinking that got us to where we are now. Most of us have not learned new processes of thinking since we were children so we must continue to learn fresh ways to think with a proven process. We all have a mindset whether it is a good one or a bad one and whether you're being influenced by a purpose or just in general by the people around you. The influences of television, being bombarded by commercials, and the ideas of those around you all have an impact. So make a conscious decision of what you want to influence your mindset. I've been told that one of the definitions of insanity is to repeat a process over and over hoping to get a different result but instead only getting the same result.

Smart Life University's goal is to give you those pieces needed to make a roadmap for your future so you're not guessing or repeating bad results. A lot of the time people muddle through life guessing on what to do to improve their lives. At Smart Life University our goal is to give you the best ideas to move yourself from point A to point B.

OPPORTUNITY

I heard a story once before that there's collectiveness in chaos. That all that was needed came together out of the chaos to form our world. All of these pieces of creation seemed to fall out of the sky in the perfect way and at the perfect time. That is Haywood Barber. That's how I got the passion for people because people had a passion for me. I love that I'm receiving so much from it as a result. I'm telling you right now that it's all about people. To help them to develop to where they want to be and what they want to do.

I grew up in the projects in New York City. You

must think I went through complete hell all the time. But it wasn't that way. I mean, I think that I had a very balanced childhood. I still did the same things we hear about Beaver and Cleaver doing or what was happening on the Andy Griffith Show. I still had that and I identified with that.

My parents were together. They're still together. It really gave me a good balance. It made me a complete person. But growing up in the projects, I learned a lot. I learned the difference between right and wrong very fast. I actually went down a lot of those paths, the wrong path a couple of times. It quickly made me aware of myself. If I wanted to live that way, it's my choice. If I wanted to live the other way, that was great too. I was good.

Opportunities are everywhere. I'm a firm believer that there are so many opportunities. We are in the 21st century. A lot of people will say there's absolutely nothing new under the sun and I'll buy that. I'll buy that in the sense that opportunities in some cases can be repackaged, an old idea that's been done before with a new slant.

I'm going to talk about slants and stacks. Slants are just simply taking an existing idea and having a new take on it. I have an example. There's a lady who wanted to provide refreshing drinks for her children that were not all sugary. This drink that she developed was simply water, filtered water with a sprinkle of fruit juice added. That idea made $300 million. That is an idea that is not new under the sun. Wouldn't you say? Now, I want everybody to understand not all ideas are going to be that simple, that easy. That was a great example of an opportunity and these types of opportunities are everywhere. Let's be clear in some cases it's just a matter of moving on the idea to bring it to life.

Smart Life University has been doing this for people and our commercial clients for years. We keep our focus on making sure you stay engaged through our processes to help you find better opportunities for yourself.

New ideas can come from almost everywhere and anywhere. New ideas come from simple places like a book, a movie, church services, workshops and seminars. At Smart Life University, we suggest books to read all the time. We suggest videos to watch because you never know when that opportunity, that idea is going to come to you. But one thing we do know is if we can get you engaged in reading, being receptive to learning, being around like minded people then we can get you and compel you to experience a whole new host of ideas and new thinking patterns. New thinking patterns lead to new opportunities. The spark is coming we just need to be ready.

I was a car salesman for a very long time. I was a car salesman making a lot of money but I was in a rut. A real rut that was very unfulfilling because I knew I had a gift inside of me to be able to teach, train and help people empower their lives. To be, do and have more of their desires. While selling cars I was doing that, I was living that but I wasn't doing it to my fullest. I did many one-on-ones, one-on-threes and so on. I was becoming a pain until they put me in management.

I developed my craft of real estate investing in the D.C. area. I had seen many people make money in real estate investing. So I started my education at the school of hard knocks and much pain. I never got it though I mean the process of connecting all of the dots to make a deal. That understanding of how I could make it my own eluded me. It finally came to me from a book and a one-on-one talk with another fairly new investor that had done her first deal.

I was making a lot of money in the car business but

I was completely broke. I was reading books in the bookstore sitting on the floor day after day. I probably went through 100 books on real estate investing. I persisted until I finally got it. The light went on about how I could take the concept of real estate investing and make it useful for me. It took me five and a half months to do my first deal but it happened after that my belief in me was born. The opportunity finally showed itself when my mindset shifted.

An opportunity is where you can actually see something that you've seen before but now you can see it in a whole different light. You can take it and mold it into the exact thing that you can use in order to reach your goal. When we change the way we see things, the way we see things change. It's like taking off sunglasses we have had on while it was getting dark outside but we hadn't noticed.

DISCIPLINE

I will tell you what discipline did in my life. I was in the car business for nearly 20 years. While I was in the car business, going through the different changes, growing into different positions and going into management the word natural leader always came up. I was a leader on the sales floor. I had different chants that I created and I would get the team revved up. I was successful as a team leader and as a manager.

I had a lot of success in the car business but I felt like I was falling into a routine outside of my passion. This was because even though the money was better and more than most average incomes it still didn't feel like I was my own man. I always wanted to be my own man. I always felt like if I was putting in that much hustle, that much work, it had to be something that was mine.

That led me to real estate investing and mortgage banking. Mortgages first, when I became a mortgage banker and learned everything there was to know about mortgages. How to put homeowners or would be homeowners into a house. That worked out very well, however it didn't pay quite enough to live off of. It did lead me to a long lost love of mine and I got better at it too. When we push towards our passion, God will make all things of the past, good or bad, relevant. He will make course corrections for us on our behalf when we start down the path of a smart life by making better decisions.

Real estate had always been an idea of mine

specifically real estate investing. At this time, there were a lot of people going around teaching about the no money down process. I was skeptical though because I'm from New York. I don't want to believe in just talk. I want to see it on paper or in real life. Not some show. One time I was conned in New York City for a lot of money and a gold diamond nameplate with a chain. That experience taught me how to analyze people and to sniff out the facts.

I went into real estate investing by way of some home courses, books, and the area investment clubs. It opened my mind up and convinced me that I could do it. Real estate investing could be done using the premise of no money down or at least no big sums of money. I dug in learned everything I could and became confident that the process would work for me.

That's really what led me to start teaching, training

and doing handholding one-on-one training. My story goes that it took me five and a half months to achieve the goal of doing one deal. Now this was after a year or two of not quite being able to grasp the concept in order to start.

Finally when I did put my foot in the water and reached out again people turned around to help me. It just seemed like the heavens opened up and made it possible. That's when I learned that energy and persistence was really not the only key. The key was taking clues from those who did deals in real estate investing already because I believe success leaves clues. Sometimes they are in the form of dirt and mud, hidden from the unaware or closed-minded. Another point is to keep a pleasing personality; this can enhance your chances of getting help.

I started hanging around the people that were successful. I went to investment clubs and real estate investment clubs. I'd actually hang around the people who were doing real deals, plus behaving different from the talkers. This is how I got on track to true success. It took me five and a half months of persisting, reading, and taking myself outside of my comfort zone. I had to be patient with myself, but firm, this is the real talk. Yes, sometimes we have talk to ourselves in a positive manner of course.

Discipline is doing the things we know that we should do that get us from point A to point B even when don't want to do them. You develop discipline by setting up structures, setting up a foundation and structures to be able to move forward from. We create structure for discipline through building blocks. I don't know if you remember when we were children and we had the ABC building blocks.

You do it in small pieces, taking your time with one piece at a time stacking and creating your structure.

With my students, I talk a lot about stacking. I told a story earlier about being in front of the cameras and not doing so well. What I realized is that I was trying to do too much at once and a lot of times we do that. What I found is that we've got to stack piece by piece. We have to take the small successes and allow them to stack up into larger successes. These traits and habits will seem hard at first but will take you to places only a few will have the pleasure of achieving.

Overall discipline will take you to the places you want to go. Just developing it over time, putting those pieces together and enjoying the successes along the way. This is another thing I found, for myself and for my students. I have catalogues of students that are statistics now of what works. What works is enjoying the successes along the way. Those successes will give you joy. Breakthroughs only come to those that push past the rejections and pain. Most people give up on the way.

We all need to know that we are accomplishing something along the way. We need to be happy with the small successes. Sometimes you're going to have setbacks but that's okay. Just keep moving forward.

My own personal disciplines are many. My number one discipline is with me losing 55 pounds to become tone. I'm going to tell you the hard facts; it was tough it took me almost 6 years.

I know people will say I don't want to do that diet because that dict is not a good diet. Most people want a 60-day diet. They want a 90-day diet. Forget about a five and a half year diet. Let me tell you though that a lot of my achievements have been done this way. Even right now I have a big goal and it's set around a seven to ten year timeframe. Using these kinds of timeframes are more real than the new popcorn microwave systems of the day or the "I want it overnight" non-sense. What do we even learn in the process if it realistically happens that way, NOTHING.

But let me go back to this goal that I had to lose weight. You know how our society is. We eat and we overeat.   I was always a slim guy but I understood that it was going to take me a while to be a slim guy again. My doctor was saying, "Alright, Mr. Barber, your blood pressure is going

up. Your cholesterol is right on the border. I see diabetes on the horizon. You're going to have to change your diet."

I said, "Alright, doc, well, what is your plan?" He said, "I don't have one for you. This is very, very simple. You are going to have to do something that you will do as a regimen." That's what I did. I did small pieces at a time that developed and became a part of my DNA, a part of my regimen. That regimen is what I live by right now. I'll tell you this, that I love light skinned Oreo cookies. I love them but because of the regimen I've developed over a period of time, I can go months without even having one.

That's what will happen in terms of discipline if you let it become a part of a habit. We know that in 21 days we can take a bad habit and replace it with a good habit. That's what I do but if you take 90 days, 100 days or a year it becomes a part of the sub-consciousness of who you are. That's what works.

The most crucial aspect of having discipline is the end result. Remember at Smart Life University we always talk about not the ABC's. We only talk about A and B. A being where you currently are. B being where you want to go. That being said, we want you to know that B is a better place than where you currently are. You've got to make sure that's established.

Of course, all these things are your choice but if you do that then they become a part of the groove of who you are. Just like now, I don't care about a Burger King Whopper even though I love them. It becomes a part of your DNA. It becomes a part of your core.

After not having a Burger King burger for over 90 days, I don't desire them that much. Now that we're talking about it, I'm probably going to want to go get one today. But I can afford to because I don't have a Burger King burger twice a week anymore.

Now, there are people that eat like that constantly. Disciplines can either be good or they can be bad. Your bad disciplines over time will cause very bad problems to develop in your life. Bad disciplines over time are going to lead to a disaster. A self-analysis will let you know where you're A is. Where you are right now.

PERSISTENCE

I've got to tell you a teachable moment is when you meet someone. They've been doing everything that they can to get across the goal post then you give them your fact-based knowledge. You learn it then you turn around and you teach it to them. You give them a blow-by-blow, a step-by-step, and you can see in their eyes right then and there, that the light turns on. This is magical for me or any other teacher.

They don't just see the light but they actually take it in. They walk with it. They run with it. And guess what. They get across the goal post. They actually make something happen. What does that do for me? It says, "This is your calling. This is your gift." So when I was in the car business I was teaching and training on the floor just because it was my nature. It was my nature to give.

They got it. It helped so many people out. When I was in the car business, I was smoking cigarettes. We'd go outside and smoke. I'd talk with the other new salesman, the rookies, and they would get it. You see the realization. The satisfaction that I was getting, the holistic feeling that it gave to my heart, that somebody got it was such a gratifying feeling. We must teach the best of what we know and have learnt at all possible turns in life always giving back. Then they're grateful.

And it happened. That was Smart Life University. Smart Life University took maybe ten years to be born going through teaching and training, and real estate investing coaching up to this day. This brought us to Smart Life University. I think of when I was putting it together with my PR people and we came up with the name. We were searching and it felt right. That's it. That was the name that we always wanted, that I always wanted, that I needed to convey to the world. It tells the whole story in a nutshell.

Nationally, we are able to help people take themselves from what I call A to B, no ABC's. I like to keep everything very simple so A to B. Where you are now is A. B is where you want to go. At Smart Life University our purpose is to just give you the A and to help you get to the B as quick as you can without losing the richness in the process. We don't have to go through the whole alphabet in

order to get you to accomplish what you want to do in your life and where you want to take yourself.

Persistence is almost everything. Persistence is

above 50% the total set of principles that you are going to need to achieve your goals. When it comes to persistence, I like to use my FFF philosophy. Sometimes it's FFF plus F.

FFF is failing, forward, fast and FFF plus F is failing, forward, fast, and frequently. It's so important that you get these failures out of the way because failing is part of the equation. A lot of people are afraid of failing but failing is the process that you need to go through in order to critique your movements, in order to succeed.

It's like driving a car. You can get on 95 and go on a straight away but would you assume that you can just take your hands off, put the steering wheel straight and just go? If you're a good driver or even a bad driver, you know you're going to have to make minor corrections along the way.

This is what I teach at Smart Life University.

You've got to make minor corrections along the way. In order to make those minor corrections; you have to fail forward fast. Failure is a part of the magic mixture. You're not going to succeed if you don't fail. You can't win or learn if you stay in the stands. We must come onto the field and play in the game to win it.

We talked about a story earlier where I stepped in front of the camera, lights, and the action and I failed. I absolutely could not get out of my own way. It was my own butt that was in the way. I was blocked. I couldn't do it. I had to make the adjustment in order to get it done. Even now, I'm explaining to you who I am and what I want to do to help you be, do, and have your goals.

If I had not gotten out of my own way, if I had not gotten out of failing, forward, fast we wouldn't be here. And I want you to do it frequently. Be okay with failing because failing is the magic elixir to get you from the A to the accomplishment that is the B. We don't do C's. We just do A and B. The way to do that simply is to persist in your failing, forward, fast, frequently. Do it. It's okay.

Richard Branson of Virgin is an excellent entrepreneur somebody to emulate. One of my satellite mentors I would say because I don't know him personally but I watch him. This guy has come up with not Coca-Cola but he's come out with soda drinks, Virgin this, and Virgin that. If you said that he had 400 ideas, 300 of them have absolutely bombed and he is real good at getting rid of them and moving on quickly.

But he's a four billion dollar success story from mediocre beginnings. Be like him fail forward fast and then every now and then repeat it frequently. Please do it.

In real estate investing, I do a lot of marketing. As

a real estate investor, I am an expert at a process called wholesaling and I'm an expert at being able to analyze deals. But let me tell you how I became an expert at analyzing deals. It was because of good marketing.

Somebody told me just yesterday, a new prospect said, "You know, I would do that real estate investing thing but it has inherent problems." It would have many problems if you do real estate investing slowly. But what we teach at Smart Life University is get through the process fast.

I was telling you about me being an expert. I am. I'm an expert at real estate investing especially at wholesaling but I'm great at analyzing deals. I become good at marketing. Let me tell you why. The best part of my marketing is that I make the phone ring. I make the process go fast so that means I'm going through deals. I'm analyzing deals. I'm talking to people because that is the number one piece that has made me an expert. The same goes for Michael Jordan he took more shots and like Hank Aaron and Babe Ruth they took more swings.

I wouldn't be an expert if I went slowly and I didn't go through the process if I'm not learning. If you go through it fast you're going to learn and this is what's going to bring you success. So, fail forward fast and you're doing it so frequently that you're learning. Your learning curve is accelerated. Many

go slow then fall off and let normal life get in the way. Then they give in to failure rather than learn from it.

The best time to persist is now. The best time to persist is immediately after a failure. Get right back on the horse. Now this is easy as easy a child riding a bike. You got on a bike. You fell off. What did Dad say, Mom say, your godfather say, and your godmother say? Get right back on. But you got a scraped up knee. You need a Band-Aid. Forget the Band-Aid. It's okay. Wipe it off. Keep on going.

Because the best time to get your understanding, to get the critical analysis of what happened and what was wrong is immediately after the failure. The main success that brought me to where I am today is that I got right back in front of the camera I was devastated but that action proved that I had won.

I have to tell you that persistence is so important that I want you to study it. I want you to be a student of persistence. I don't want you to ever give up on the execution of what persistence is. You have to persist. Never give up on persistence. That is what brings it all together. It will give you the opportunity to figure out where you went wrong in order to go forward to win. And at Smart Life University we want you to win.

THE SURROUNDING FIVE

For me to typecast my students would be very tough because all of their different types of backgrounds. You know America is a melting pot and I've had the privilege of teaching people from India, Asia, Africa, all around this country and all parts of the world.

People from my exact background, I've been able to help. People that have already had a good measure of success I've been able to help. These people I love to help because they already understand the concept of business. They already understand the concept of achieving greater. Knowing the fact that they are taking themselves from a place of "Alright, I have three revenue streams but I would like to add another one. Are there any other good ideas?" is exhilarating. When we learn the process of success, it is very simple to rinse and repeat it over and over again.

Which I think is a good concept in life. If you can stack your life with more and more good stuff, then at the end of the day, you have a smart life. That's only because you're stacking yourself with good stuff. Those people that are fully aware that they want more. They see more and they know that more is available. Those people their backgrounds do vary sometimes they are very poor but they already understand that there is a gift in them and it just needs to be developed.

People come to me all the time and say, "I'm this close but I don't know how to get over the line." Smart Life University has a way to get over that line. The process is simple. I don't ever want to make anybody walk away with just easy but with simple. We make it very step-by-step, a methodical process the experience is unlike anything else that they've ever experienced in any teaching capacity.

I'm of a belief that this should be instituted in school, maybe colleges and universities because what I do is I make them feel like somebody is actually right on their shoulder.

I'm holding their hand. I make them feel as comfortable as possible through some of the pitfalls where I didn't have someone holding my hand. I want them to have what I was missing.

What I've given in my training is what I wish I had month one even though it took me five and a half months to complete. What I'm giving them is handholding every single step of the way.

Surrounding five is so critical. I wrote about persistence earlier as being a strong percentage. Well, the next strong percentage is the surrounding five. It's been said that our sum total of who are and even our income is the average of the five surrounding people that we are the closest to. This is our average income. If that is true then it has to be true that also our overall attitude our base disciplines, our base thought philosophy, has to be almost the same thing because you're attracted to the people that you're around.

We're all magnets that is what we are. It's very critical for us to make sure that the surrounding five are people at our level or higher. When I say our level, I want you to understand you don't want to be the smartest person in the room.

I have a best friend. Actually, I even have a child of mine that says that he's the smartest person in his group. Well, let me tell you if that's the case that's a sad statement to ever make never be that person. You want to be in a group or mastermind group where you maybe the low to middle brainpower, so you can ABL (always be learning). Good students like good teachers are always learning. Please don't be ashamed to study and learn, trust me it will separate you from the pack. The surrounding five is very important.

What I do is I read a lot of books. I read a lot of biographies so I'm always assessing people based on those biographies. I read about Edison. I read about Ford. I read about Michael Jordan. I read about all the successful people that I want learn from and then I use their criteria of who they are now at their highest success. I use that as the measurement of the people I want around me. I want to make sure that everyone's always going for their best and then I know they can come into my inner circle.

The inner circle is so important it is very critical to make sure those people are at the highest level they can be. The people in my top five are people that are open to new ideas, new people with good ideas, and people that are successful that have done a lot of overcoming.

It doesn't mean right this second you have to have a mansion, a big house and a great car none of that matters. Let me tell you, I've been through two fortunes. I've made some critical mistakes in spending money. Now I have to have a CPA watch my dollars and cents. How silly is that, right? But if you want to be rich and you want to have the most successful life, you have to cut off the things that are sucking you dry.

The people around me have to be the people that are doing the things that I am doing or doing the things that I know that I need to do. We go back to disciplines. I have a lot of disciplines. I've used a lot of disciplines to succeed to get to where I currently am. However, I still have disciplines that I have to master in order to be my better self.

Success is not a destination. It's an overall journey. So, I'm still on my journey. I have more people to help. I have more people that I want to bring into my team and bring into my family that I can show them how to get from A to B. Smart Life University is not a place where we are just comfortable and we're going to stay here and take it easy. We're here to instruct, teach, and train people to get to their highest self and that's what we're going to do forever.

The surrounding five is critical. The focus of creating your best surrounding five is to develop your network. They become your team. They become your mastermind. Just like being involved with Smart Life University. Simply put on a day-today basis having a good surrounding five is crucial. We all drip on each other good positivity, good energy, good love, and good support.

What are you doing today in order to improve from yesterday? See all these things are a part of the principles, the procedures and the processes that make you have a smart life, have a better life.

The people that are not in my top five, I avoid them like the plague. I want to tell you why. Not that they're not nice people. In most cases, they are nice

people. But it's not congruent with where I'm going and what I'm doing. I mean, I've had a lot of accomplishments in my life. I want you to understand, I'm not bragging but I'm trying to impress upon you a point of what you can do. I've had a lot of things that could have become stumbling blocks that could have stopped me from moving forward.

I don't know where you are, what you're doing, and what's in your way but I want you to know that if you have the good people around that help you and support you success is possible. The surrounding five is a network. It's a mastermind.

Just like we talk about Smart Life University doing the same thing but we do it in a massive way. Our chat room has massive amounts of people talking back and forth. We are always sending out good vibes, sending out good energy. Always believing that you are going to be great in your achievements. That's why it's so important that we make sure that we bring the right people around us all the time.

Haywood Barber

LIVE SMART

My mission, my purpose, my quest in life as I've developed into this man, into this leader, is to become the best leader. That teacher that helps people get to their ultimate purpose that they wished for. Because by the time a person gets to me, I can see it.

I interview every single person before they actually sign up for my program. I have to make sure that I see that potential that eye of the tiger. At least that they won't quit as long as they know they've got the right blueprint and that's what I provide. It feels good. The mission is to get this information into as many that are willing to step in the ring knowing that they have the biggest secret, which is the knockout punch, to win.

A smart life is the sum total of all the principles in this book. My smart life comes from my dumb life.

Now, I'm not talking about you at all because I don't want to be the judge of you. But what I am here to do and what Smart Life University is here to do is to give you the selection. Just like going into any supermarket. Go into any supermarket and there's a plethora of foods, junk food, good food, medium food, fattening foods, and cholesterol rich foods. You have your choice.

What Smart Life University is here for is to give you your choice. Now, we're only going to offer good choices for you to pick from. The thinking, the philosophy behind Smart Life University is for you. You can come here and get your best in order to stack into your life. Right now you're reading about a Haywood Barber that has made more mistakes than you because I've made a whole bunch.

I assure you that if you talked to my mother 30 years ago she would have said, "That guy, he might be ambitious but he's not going anywhere because he makes a lot of dumb moves." And I did for a long time until I was introduced to some ideas, a philosophy, and a thought process that made me better. That's my goal here. Now, you don't have to do it but this is here for you to make good choices to have a smart life.

A smart life is better than what I had a dumb life. I want this for you. It's designed for you. It's designed for your children. It's designed for you to make better decisions in your day-to-day life. I

learned a long time ago from one of my mentors to work harder on myself than on my job. In order to move and separate myself from the 97% of other people, to become a part of the 3% of unique people it had to be a choice of calculated decisions of who you want to be and who you want to gather around yourself.

Smart Life that's what we do. We bring it in for you to have the right stuff. Now, it's a lot of information and I don't suggest that you try to suck it all up at once. Let Smart Life University, let our website, let what we do be a routine. We're going to make sure you have books. We're going to make sure you have video. We're going to make sure that we point you in directions of the good stuff.

Why? To help you achieve a good life, that's our mission and I want you to become a part of our mission. Now, you don't have to but if you want to teach and train you can. I'm a firm believer this is my philosophy in life that everything that I learn I want to turn back around and teach to others. If we are moving this way together as a team of teachers and trainers for a good life, for a smart life, then we could change the direction of the whole country maybe even the whole world. If we move that way and for the benefit of all we must.

I don't know anything about sports. I tell you guys all the time. I make analogies with sports but sometimes I can get lost because I really don't

know that much about football, basketball, baseball, golf, swimming, or anything. Nothing. But here we go. If we can be fans of our children the way we are fans for hockey, world soccer, Super Bowl Sunday, regular Monday night football, baseball, they can achieve anything.

If we can be a fan of our children giving them this type of information, telling them about finances, teaching them about a smart life then we can actually change them from going through some of the pitfalls that I've gone through and perhaps you've gone through. We need to teach our children how to have a smart life early so that they can start off on the right track.

Smart Life University is about you, it is about getting you to point B where you want to be from point A where you are. If we can do that for you and your children, it will make a difference. I promise you. My mission through Smart Life University is to calculate, assess, use statistics on that. We mentioned the 97% where most people are winding up and then changing that trajectory.

Most people don't know where their retirement is going to take them because they are afraid to look at it. We have people in their 30's, 40's, 50's that are counting on a system that's been broken for 30 years. At Smart Life University, we're here to make sure that you are fully aware of the reality of what exists and how it can help you.

Let me say this. One thing that I am sure of is that you can count on yourself. If I put the responsibility on you, I can show you how to take that responsibility. To know where you're going to wind up so you know where you're going to be for sure it changes the whole way that you move, and how you walk on a daily basis. A smart life builds confidence. It gives you confidence in how you move.

So many people today are not sure of where they're going. They don't know where they're going to wind up. They're not sure if Social Security is going to be available or not. Matter of fact I can assure you if you're below 30 it won't exist for you. And if you are above 30 it is suspect whether it will still exist.

At Smart Life University we want to make sure we give you a crystal clear idea of where you're going to wind up. Then you can make the decision about what you want to have. Do you want to have a rich retirement, do you want to have a sub-par retirement or even do you want to go rudderless and not know? Do you want to be a meaningful specific or do you want to be a wandering generality? It's all up to you.

But at Smart Life University, this is our job and we are accomplishing this job because we have success stories now. We're making sure that we're putting the right plate on the table. So, for you it's either super rich diet for your mind and yourself or a super fast track. We're only putting good stuff on the table. That's it. We're not putting soft, bad choices. You're only going to have the greatest choices possible.

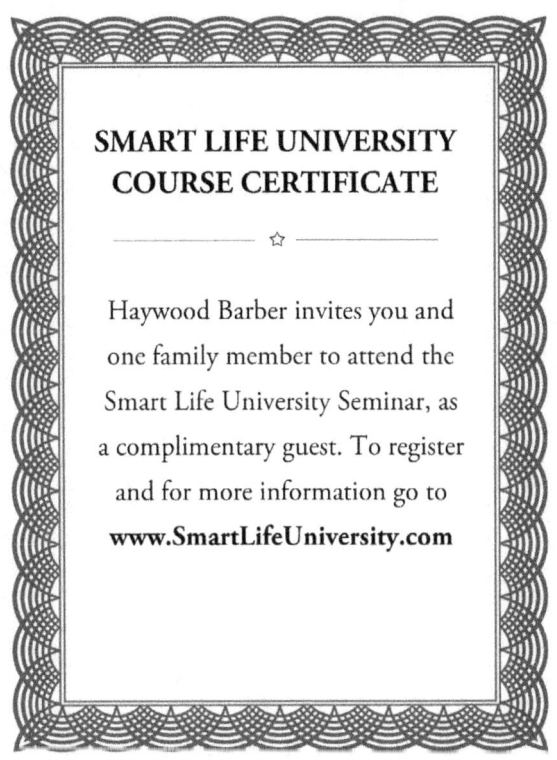

SMART LIFE UNIVERSITY
COURSE CERTIFICATE

☆

Haywood Barber invites you and
one family member to attend the
Smart Life University Seminar, as
a complimentary guest. To register
and for more information go to
www.SmartLifeUniversity.com

VISION

My end result, my goal, my vision, what I see at the
end of the day when I finalize my time here, is to
know that I have helped as many people as possible.
The ones that want it and they want it bad but they
just don't know how to accomplish it. With my help
now they know they have it inside them to succeed
and win at will.